Bouba & Zaza
make peace

ADEA
Association for the Development of Education in Africa

Michel LAFON EDUCATION

UNESCO
United Nations Educational, Scientific and Cultural Organization

One morning, Bouba arrived at school with a boy whom nobody else knew.
"This is my new cousin," he said to Zaza. "His name is Yao. There is war in his country."
"Oh dear, you are not very lucky," said Zaza. "That's horrible! What is war really like?"
Yao did not answer.
"Don't you talk? Hey, Bouba, has he lost his tongue?" asked Zaza.
"You know, Zaza," murmured Bouba, "I don't know him very well. It was my dad who told me to be nice to him. But you are right, he doesn't say much!"

At break time the children wanted to interrogate the new boy.
"What is war?"
"War is when grown-ups fight with weapons and there are people who die," replied Hamidou.
"Oh, I see. So, did you fight in a war like the grown-ups, Yao? Did you kill anyone? Did you have a weapon? Were you scared? Did you see blood? Did you see any dead bodies, any injuries? Is it really true that when there is a war you don't have a house any more and there is nothing left to eat? Were you hungry? Where did you sleep? Why aren't you dead? Did you get out all by yourself? And where are your parents? And your bothers and sisters?"
Yao did not reply to any of the questions and Zaza intervened.
"Stop! He probably doesn't want to talk about it at the moment!"

After school, Bouba asked Yao if he would like to play football: "But before we play I have to tell you something. Two groups argue over the football pitch. My lot say that the pitch is ours because it is in our part of town; the others say it is theirs because they filled the holes in the pitch and made the goals. You are in my group because you are living with me. OK, let's go, shall we?"

But instead of answering, Yao just sat at the foot of a tree. He seemed to be angry. Bouba was a little disappointed but he decided he did not want to force Yao to play.

"Bouba, why doesn't your cousin come onto the pitch?" said Koffi. "You told him about our problem, didn't you? If he doesn't come with us it means that he is with the other group – against us. And his family and friends are also against us. They are our enemies!"
Bouba did not really see what Yao's family and friends had to do with the argument, but he did not say anything to his friends because he really wanted to play football.

"Hey Bouba, why didn't you pass? Are you playing on your own? Get back on the subs' bench and stay there!" said Koffi.
Koffi was a leader. He was only seven years old but he looked more like ten.
"I could have scored if you had not been pulling my shirt!" said Bouba. "I have had enough of you giving me orders, you are not my father!"
"I am the boss," replied Koffi, pushing Bouba violently. "An order is an order!"
And that was when Yao leaped up, caught Koffi by his shirt and shouted: "Do not touch him again or I will kill you!"
It took the whole group to make Yao let go of Koffi's shirt. Bouba really could not understand his new cousin. At night he shouted in his sleep and during the day he did not say a word. Nonetheless when Bouba was attacked he could not stand it.
"I must talk to Dad about this," thought Bouba.

"Dad, Dad, only you can help me. You are a lawyer so you must know how to defend people, right?"
"What is it, Bouba? Who needs to be defended?"
"Nobody likes Yao. He doesn't say anything, he's violent and I am going to end up losing all my friends."
"Bouba, when they play 'war', lots of children think it's fun, because at the end of the game they go home, see their parents and have dinner. Yao saw his family and his friends die. He doesn't have a house any more. His school was destroyed. He needs help but he also needs time to get back to living a normal life!"
Bouba did not say anything but he asked himself how he could help Yao and keep his own friends too.

That night, Yao was screaming. All the children woke with a start. Bouba tried to calm Yao who, still in the grip of his nightmare, was fighting and punching and kicking as if defending himself.

“Yao, it’s me, Bouba. Stop it, calm down! Mum, come and help me!” Eventually, Yao woke up. He looked at all the children around him and at Bouba’s mum. His heart was beating very fast. He was scared but he did not say anything. He went back to sleep on his mat with his head in his hands.

The next day, Bouba was still disturbed by the night so he didn't dare to talk to Yao. But he wanted to make up with his friends.
"What if we made peace? We had more fun before!"
"You are just a coward! You're scared of fighting," said Koffi.
"I'm not scared. I just said that we had more fun when we all played together."
"Fine then. You're not part of our team any more!"

After that, Bouba still went with Yao to the football pitch. The two teams were often face to face. Quickly the pitch became a battle ground. They were insulting each other, threatening each other and making signs. Then one day the violence started. The smallest children tried to hide behind the bigger ones. Suddenly Yao shouted out and the fighting stopped. Sylvestre was lying on the ground. Blood was pouring across his cheek. He was not moving.

In an instant, everyone disappeared. Only Bouba, Yao and a few other children surrounded the injured child. "Sylvestre, you aren't dead, are you? I mean really dead? Answer me!" cried Bouba. "Zaza, go and get help, quickly!" Luckily Zaza lived close to the pitch and her mother was a nurse.

Very quickly, Zaza's mother organized help. Sylvestre had to go to hospital. Yao, Bouba and Zaza watched the ambulance drive away. The children were terrified. What would happen to Sylvestre?

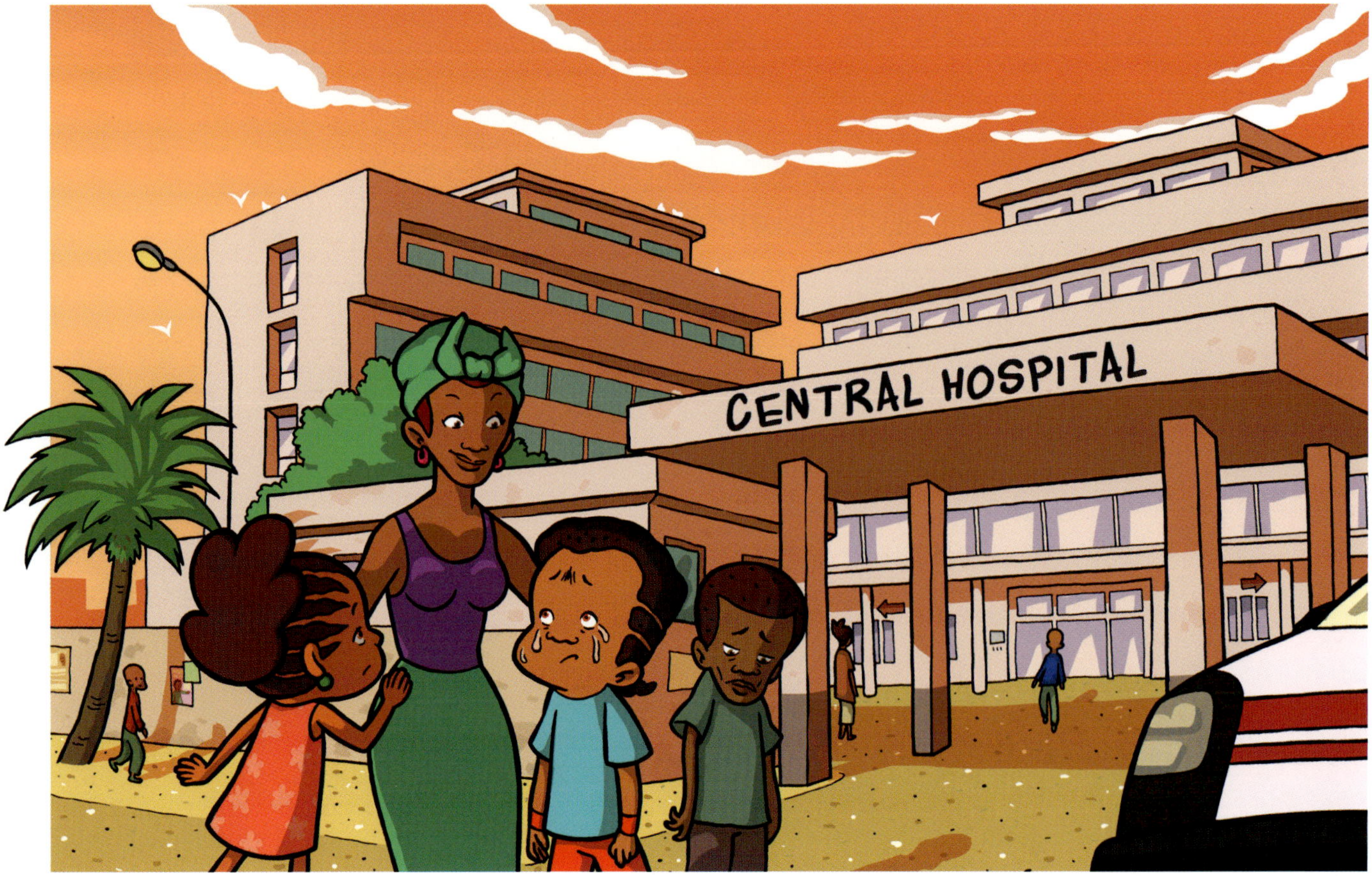

It was nearly night, and the children were still waiting outside the hospital. At last, Zaza's mother came out to give them the news. "Sylvestre nearly lost an eye. He must stay in hospital for a few days. I hope this drama will be a good lesson for everyone. Your headmaster has decided to get everybody together in the playground tomorrow morning to put and end to this violence once and for all."

"Oh Auntie, I am so sad. I couldn't calm down my friends, there was nothing I could do. Poor Sylvestre! And also poor Yao, who just really needs to hear people laughing."

Next day, the headmaster's speech was understood by all. And one month later, as the referee blew the final whistle, the players shook hands and swapped shirts. The Leopard team had just beaten the Lions by two goals to one. The victors made a lap of honour. It was Sylvestre, the team's goalkeeper, who carried the cup. Suddenly he called to the captain of the lions, his former enemy.

"Koffi, that was a great match, wasn't it?"

"Yes, it was really magnificent. And I look forward to next Sunday for revenge. Come on – my mother has made us all some nice food."

After Sylvestre came back, the children at the school did not fight any more. They prefer to play, dance and sing together. Yao, too, seems happy. He talks to everyone and joins in if there is a party. The other day he even said that there had been a big storm that brought him to the land of peace.

Illustrations: Thomas Penin